My Very First Layette

Designer details provide heirloom quality to these precious outfits and blankets for newborns. Choose from four styles in lightweight yarn for girls and boys.

SHOPPING LIST

Yarn (Light Weight)

[5 ounces, 459 yards
(141 grams, 420 meters) per skein]:

☐ Pink - 5 skeins
☐ White - 1 skein

Crochet Hook

☐ Size F (3.75 mm)
   or size needed for gauge

Additional Supplies

☐ Yarn needle
☐ Sewing needle and thread
☐ ³⁄₈" (10 mm) Buttons - 3 for
   Sacque

GAUGE INFORMATION

13 sc and 15 rows = 3" (7.5 cm)
   In pattern,
   3 repeats = 4¼" (10.75 cm)
Gauge Swatch: 3" (7.5 cm) square
Ch 14.
Row 1: Sc in second ch from hook
and in each ch across.
Rows 2-15: Ch 1, turn; sc in each sc
across.
Finish off.

——STITCH GUIDE——

SHELL
(3 Dc, ch 1, 3 dc) in sc indicated.
▥ PICOT
Ch 3, slip st in top of sc just made.
▥ CLUSTER (uses next 5 sts)
† YO, skip next dc, insert hook in **next**
dc, YO and pull up a loop, YO and
draw through 2 loops on hook †, YO,
insert hook in next Picot, YO and pull
up a loop, repeat from † to † once, YO
and draw through all 5 loops on hook.
▥ SINGLE CROCHET 2 TOGETHER
(abbreviated sc2tog)
Pull up a loop in each of next 2 sts, YO
and draw through all 3 loops on hook
(counts as one sc).
▥ ENDING DECREASE
(uses last 3 sts)
YO, insert hook in next dc, YO and
pull up a loop, YO and draw through
2 loops on hook, YO twice, skip next
dc, insert hook in last sc, YO and pull
up a loop, (YO and draw through
2 loops on hook) twice, YO and draw
through all 3 loops on hook.

SACQUE
YOKE

With White, ch 56.

Row 1: Sc in second ch from hook
and in each ch across: 55 sc.

Row 2 (Right side)**:** Ch 1, turn; sc in
each sc across.

Note: Loop a short piece of yarn
around any stitch to mark Row 2 as
right side.

Row 3: Ch 1, turn; sc in first 2 sc, 2 sc
in next sc, (sc in next 2 sc, 2 sc in next
sc) across to last sc, sc in last sc: 73 sc.

Rows 4-6: Ch 1, turn; sc in each
sc across.

Row 7: Ch 1, turn; sc in first 2 sc, 2 sc
in next sc, (sc in next 3 sc, 2 sc in next
sc) across to last 2 sc, sc in last 2 sc:
91 sc.

Rows 8-10: Ch 1, turn; sc in each
sc across.

Row 11: Ch 1, turn; sc in first 3 sc, 2 sc
in next sc, (sc in next 4 sc, 2 sc in next
sc) across to last 2 sc, sc in last 2 sc:
109 sc.

Rows 12 and 13: Ch 1, turn; sc in each
sc across.

Row 14: Ch 4 (**counts as first dc plus
ch 1**), turn; skip next sc, dc in next
sc, ★ ch 1, skip next sc, dc in next sc;
repeat from ★ across; finish off: 55 dc
and 54 ch-1 sps.

BODY

Row 1: With **wrong** side facing, join Pink with sc in first dc *(see Joining With Sc, page 30)*; 2 sc in next ch-1 sp and in next dc, † sc in next ch-1 sp and in next dc, 2 sc in next ch-1 sp, sc in next dc and in next ch-1 sp, 2 sc in next dc †; repeat from † to † once **more**, place marker around last dc worked into for st placement, ch 7, skip next 11 dc (armhole), (2 sc in next dc, sc in next ch-1 sp, sc in next dc and in next ch-1 sp) 4 times, sc in next dc, (sc in next ch-1 sp, sc in next dc and in next ch-1 sp, 2 sc in next dc) 4 times, place marker around last dc worked into for st placement, ch 7, skip next 11 dc (armhole), 2 sc in next dc, repeat from † to † twice, 2 sc in next ch-1 sp, sc in last dc: 83 sc and 14 chs.

Row 2: Ch 1, turn; sc in first sc, skip next 3 sc, work Shell in next sc, skip next 3 sc, sc in next sc, ★ work Picot, skip next 3 sts, work Shell in next sc, skip next 3 sts, sc in next st; repeat from ★ across: 13 sc and 12 Shells.

Row 3: Ch 3, turn; skip first 2 sts, dc in next dc, ch 3, 2 sc in next ch-1 sp, ch 3, ★ work Cluster, ch 3, 2 sc in next ch-1 sp, ch 3; repeat from ★ across to last 4 sts, skip next dc, work ending decrease: 24 ch-3 sps.

Row 4: Ch 1, turn; sc in first st, work Shell in next sc, skip next sc and next 2 chs, sc in next ch, ★ work Picot, skip next Cluster and next 3 chs, work Shell in next sc, skip next sc and next 2 chs, sc in next ch; repeat from ★ across, leave remaining dc unworked: 13 sc and 12 Shells.

Rows 5-14: Repeat Rows 3 and 4, 5 times.

Finish off.

SLEEVE

Rnd 1: With **wrong** side facing, join Pink with sc in free loop of center ch at underarm *(Fig. 3b, page 31)*; sc in next 2 chs, pull up a loop in next ch and in marked dc on Yoke, YO and draw through all 3 loops on hook, pull up a loop in next ch-1 sp and in next dc, YO and draw through all 3 loops on hook, sc in next ch-1 sp and in next dc, 2 sc in next ch-1 sp, sc in next dc, (sc in next ch-1 sp and in next dc) twice, (2 sc in next ch-1 sp, sc in next dc) twice, (sc in next ch-1 sp and in next dc) twice, 2 sc in next ch-1 sp, sc in next dc and in next ch-1 sp, pull up a loop in next dc and in next ch-1 sp, YO and draw through all 3 loops on hook, pull up a loop in next dc on Yoke and in next ch at armhole, YO and draw through all 3 loops on hook, sc in last 2 chs; join with slip st to first sc: 32 sts.

Rnd 2: Ch 3 (**counts as first dc, now and throughout**), turn; 2 dc in same st, skip next 3 sts, sc in next st, work Picot, skip next 3 sts, ★ work Shell in next sc, skip next 3 sts, sc in next st, work Picot, skip next 3 sts; repeat from ★ 2 times **more**, 3 dc in same st as first dc, ch 1; join with slip st to first dc: 4 Picots and 4 Shells.

Rnd 3: Ch 1, turn; 2 sc in first ch-1 sp, ch 3, work Cluster, ch 3, ★ 2 sc in next ch-1 sp, ch 3, work Cluster, ch 3; repeat from ★ 2 times **more**; join with slip st to first sc: 8 ch-3 sps.

Rnd 4: Slip st in next sc, ch 3, turn; 2 dc in same st, skip next sc and next 2 chs, sc in next ch, work Picot, skip next Cluster and next 3 chs, ★ work Shell in next sc, skip next sc and next 2 chs, sc in next ch, work Picot, skip next Cluster and next 3 chs; repeat from ★ 2 times **more**, 3 dc in same st as first dc, ch 1; join with slip st to first dc: 4 Picots and 4 Shells.

Rnds 5-12: Repeat Rnds 3 and 4, 4 times.

Rnd 13: Ch 1, turn; sc in first ch-1 sp, ch 3, work Cluster, ch 3, ★ sc in next ch-1 sp, ch 3, work Cluster, ch 3; repeat from ★ 2 times **more**; join with slip st to first sc, finish off: 8 ch-3 sps.

Rnd 14: With **right** side facing, join White with sc in first ch-3 sp after joining; sc in same sp and in next Cluster, (2 sc in each of next 2 ch-3 sps, sc in next Cluster) 3 times, 2 sc in last ch-3 sp; join with slip st to first sc.

Rnd 15: Ch 1, do **not** turn; sc in same st and in each sc around; join with slip st to first sc, finish off.

Repeat for second Sleeve.

RIGHT FRONT BAND

Row 1: With **right** side facing and working in end of rows, join Pink with sc in Row 14 of Body; 3 sc in next row, sc in next row, 2 sc in next row, ★ sc in next row, 3 sc in next row, sc in next row, 2 sc in next row; repeat from ★ once **more**, sc in next 2 rows, 2 sc in next row, sc in next 3 rows, skip next row, sc in next 5 rows, skip next row, sc in last 3 rows: 36 sc.

Row 2 (Buttonhole row): Ch 1, turn; sc in first sc, ch 1, skip next sc, ★ sc in next 4 sc, ch 1, skip next sc; repeat from ★ once **more**, sc in last 24 sc.

Row 3: Ch 1, turn; sc in each sc and in each ch across; finish off.

LEFT FRONT BAND

Row 1: With **right** side facing and working in end of rows, join Pink with sc in Row 1 of Yoke; sc in next 2 rows, skip next row, sc in next 5 rows, skip next row, sc in next 3 rows, 2 sc in next row, sc in next 2 rows, ★ 2 sc in next row, sc in next row, 3 sc in next row, sc in next row; repeat from ★ 2 times **more**: 36 sc.

Rows 2 and 3: Ch 1, turn; sc in each sc across.

Finish off.

NECK EDGING

Row 1: With **wrong** side facing and working in end of rows on Front Bands and in free loops of beginning ch on Yoke, join Pink with sc in Row 3 of Left Front Band; sc in next 2 rows and in next ch, (sc2tog, sc in next ch) 18 times, sc in last 3 rows: 43 sc.

Row 2: Ch 1, turn; sc in each sc across.

Row 3: Ch 1, turn; working in  Back Loops Only *(Fig. 1, page 30)*, slip st in first 3 sc, sc in next sc, work Picot, ★ skip next sc, work Shell in next sc, skip next sc, sc in next sc, work Picot; repeat from ★ across to last 3 sc, slip st in last 3 sc.

Row 4: Ch 1, turn; working in free loops *(Fig. 3a, page 31)* and in Back Loops Only of skipped sc on Row 2, sc in each sc across; finish off.

Sew buttons to Left Front Band opposite buttonholes.

CAP

Rnd 1 (Right side): With White, ch 2, 6 sc in second ch from hook; join with slip st to first sc: 6 sc.

Note: Loop a short piece of yarn around any stitch to mark Rnd 1 as **right** side.

Rnd 2: Ch 1, 2 sc in same st and in each sc around; join with slip st to first sc: 12 sc.

Rnd 3: Ch 1, sc in same st and in each sc around; join with slip st to first sc.

Rnds 4 and 5: Repeat Rnds 2 and 3: 24 sc.

Rnd 6: Ch 1, sc in same st, 2 sc in next sc, (sc in next sc, 2 sc in next sc) around; join with slip st to first sc: 36 sc.

Rnd 7: Ch 1, sc in same st and in each sc around; join with slip st to first sc.

Rnd 8: Ch 1, sc in same st and in next sc, 2 sc in next sc, (sc in next 2 sc, 2 sc in next sc) around; join with slip st to first sc: 48 sc.

Rnd 9: Ch 1, sc in same st and in each sc around; join with slip st to first sc.

Rnd 10: Ch 1, sc in same st and in next 2 sc, 2 sc in next sc, (sc in next 3 sc, 2 sc in next sc) around; join with slip st to first sc: 60 sc.

Rnds 11-20: Ch 1, sc in same st and in each sc around; join with slip st to first sc.

Rnd 21: Ch 1, **turn**; sc in same st and in each sc around; join with slip st to first sc.

Rnd 22: Ch 1, do **not** turn; sc in same st and in each sc around; join with slip st to first sc, finish off.

EDGING

Rnd 1: With **wrong** side facing, join Pink with slip st in any sc; ch 3 (**counts as first dc, now and throughout**), 2 dc in same st, skip next 2 sc, sc in next sc, work Picot, skip next 2 sc, ★ work Shell in next sc, skip next 2 sc, sc in next sc, work Picot, skip next 2 sc; repeat from ★ around, 3 dc in same st as first dc, ch 1; join with slip st to first dc: 10 Picots and 10 Shells.

Rnd 2: Ch 1, turn; 2 sc in first ch-1 sp, ch 3, work Cluster, ch 3, ★ 2 sc in next ch-1 sp, ch 3, work Cluster, ch 3; repeat from ★ around; join with slip st to first sc: 20 ch-3 sps.

Rnd 3: Slip st in next sc, ch 3, turn; 2 dc in same st, skip next sc and next 2 chs, sc in next ch, work Picot, skip next Cluster and next 3 chs, ★ work Shell in next sc, skip next sc and next 2 chs, sc in next ch, work Picot, skip next Cluster and next 3 chs; repeat from ★ around, 3 dc in same st as first dc, ch 1; join with slip st to first dc, finish off.

With Pink, make a 📹 pom-pom *(Figs. 5a-c, page 31)* and sew to top of Cap. Turn Edging up.

BOOTIES
SOLE

With Pink, ch 10.

Rnd 1 (Right side)**:** 3 Sc in second ch from hook, sc in next 7 chs, 5 sc in last ch; working in 📹 free loops of beginning ch *(Fig. 3b, page 31)*, sc in next 7 chs, 2 sc in same ch as first sc; join with slip st to first sc: 24 sc.

Note: Loop a short piece of yarn around any stitch to mark Rnd 1 as **right** side.

Rnd 2: Ch 1, 2 sc in same st, sc in next sc, 2 sc in next sc, sc in next 7 sc, 2 sc in next sc, (sc in next sc, 2 sc in next sc) twice, sc in next 7 sc, 2 sc in next sc, sc in last sc; join with slip st to first sc: 30 sc.

Rnd 3: Ch 1, sc in same st and in next sc, † 2 sc in next sc, sc in next sc, 2 sc in next sc, sc in next 7 sc, 2 sc in next sc, sc in next sc, 2 sc in next sc †, sc in next 2 sc, repeat from † to † once; join with slip st to first sc: 38 sc.

Rnd 4: Ch 1, sc in same st and in each sc around; join with slip st to 📹 Back Loop Only of first sc *(Fig. 1, page 30)*; do **not** finish off.

Rnd 1: Ch 1, sc in Back Loop Only of same st and each sc around; join with slip st to **both** loops of first sc, finish off.

Rnd 2: With **right** side facing and working in both loops, 📹 join White with sc in same st as joining *(see Joining With Sc, page 30)*; sc in next sc and in each sc around; join with slip st to first sc.

Rnds 3 and 4: Ch 1, sc in same st and in each sc around; join with slip st to first sc.

Rnd 5: Ch 1, sc in same st and in next 15 sc, sc2tog, sc in next sc, sc2tog twice, sc in next sc, sc2tog, sc in last 12 sc; join with slip st to first sc: 34 sc.

Rnd 6: Ch 1, sc in same st and in next 14 sc, sc2tog, (sc in next sc, sc2tog) twice, sc in last 11 sc; join with slip st to first sc: 31 sc.

Rnd 7: Ch 1, sc in same st and in next 13 sc, sc2tog, pull up a loop in next 3 sc, YO and draw through all 4 loops on hook, sc2tog, sc in last 10 sc; join with slip st to first sc: 27 sts.

Rnd 8: Ch 1, sc in same st and in next 11 sc, sc2tog, pull up a loop in each of next 3 sts, YO and draw through all 4 loops on hook, sc2tog, sc in last 8 sc; join with slip st to first sc: 23 sts.

Rnd 9: Ch 1, sc in same st and in next 10 sc, sc2tog 3 times, sc in last 6 sc; join with slip st to first sc, do **not** finish off: 20 sc.

CUFF

Rnds 1-3: Ch 1, sc in same st and in each sc around; join with slip st to first sc.

Finish off.

Rnd 4: With **right** side facing and working in Back Loops Only, join Pink with sc in same st as joining; sc in each sc around; join with slip st to **both** loops of first sc.

Rnd 5: Ch 1, sc in both loops of same st and each sc around; join with slip st to first sc, finish off.

Rnd 6: With **right** side facing, top of Cuff toward you, and working in  free loops of sc on Rnd 3 *(Fig. 3a, page 31)*, join Pink with sc in first sc before joining; work Picot, skip next sc, work Shell in next sc, skip next sc, ★ sc in next sc, work Picot, skip next sc, work Shell in next sc, skip next sc; repeat from ★ around; join with slip st to first sc, finish off.

AFGHAN

Finished Size: 34" x 48"
  (86.5 cm x 122 cm)

AFGHAN BODY

With Pink, ch 186.

Row 1 (Right side)**:** Sc in second ch from hook, skip next 3 chs, work Shell in next ch, ★ skip next 3 chs, sc in next ch, work Picot, skip next 3 chs, work Shell in next ch; repeat from ★ across to last 4 chs, skip next 3 chs, sc in last ch: 24 sc and 23 Shells.

Note: Loop a short piece of yarn around any stitch to mark Row 1 as **right** side.

Row 2: Ch 3, turn; skip first 2 sts, dc in next dc, ch 3, 2 sc in next ch-1 sp, ch 3, ★ work Cluster, ch 3, 2 sc in next ch-1 sp, ch 3; repeat from ★ across to last 4 sts, skip next dc, work ending decrease: 46 ch-3 sps.

Row 3: Ch 1, turn; sc in first st, work Shell in next sc, skip next sc and next 2 chs, sc in next ch, ★ work Picot, skip next Cluster and next 3 chs, work Shell in next sc, skip next sc and next 2 chs, sc in next ch; repeat from ★ across, leave remaining dc unworked: 24 sc and 23 Shells.

Repeat Rows 2 and 3 until Afghan Body measures approximately 46" (117 cm) from beginning ch, ending by working Row 3.

Last Row: Ch 3, turn; skip first 2 sts, dc in next dc, ch 3, sc in next ch-1 sp, ch 3, ★ work Cluster, ch 3, sc in next ch-1 sp, ch 3; repeat from ★ across to last 4 sts, skip next dc, work ending decrease; finish off: 46 ch-3 sps.

EDGING

Rnd 1: With **wrong** side facing,  join White with sc in first dc on Last Row *(see Joining With Sc, page 30)*; sc in same st, 2 sc in next ch-3 sp, (sc in next st, 2 sc in next ch-3 sp) across to last st, 3 sc in last st; work 191 sc  evenly spaced across end of rows; working in  free loops *(Fig. 3b, page 31)* and in sps across beginning ch, 3 sc in ch at base of first sc, 2 sc in next sp, (sc in next ch, 2 sc in next sp) across to last ch, 3 sc in last ch; work 191 sc evenly spaced across end of rows; sc in same st as first sc; join with slip st to first sc: 668 sc.

Rnd 2: Ch 1, turn; 2 sc in same st, sc in each sc around working 3 sc in center sc of each corner 3-sc group, sc in same st as first sc; join with slip st to first sc: 676 sc.

Rnd 3: Ch 3, do **not** turn; (2 dc, ch 1, 3 dc) in same st, † ★ skip next sc, sc in next sc, work Picot, (skip next 2 sc, work Shell in next sc, skip next 2 sc, sc in next sc, work Picot) across to next corner 3-sc group, skip next sc †, work Shell in next sc; repeat from ★ 2 times **more**, then repeat from † to † once; join with slip st to top of beginning ch-3, finish off.

Green Set

SHOPPING LIST

Yarn (Light Weight)

[5 ounces, 459 yards
(141 grams, 420 meters) per
skein]:

- ☐ Green - 4 skeins
- ☐ White - 2 skeins

Crochet Hook

- ☐ Size F (3.75 mm)
  or size needed for gauge

Additional Supplies

- ☐ Safety pins - 2
- ☐ Yarn needle
- ☐ Sewing needle and thread
- ☐ ³⁄₈" (10 mm) Buttons - 5 for
  Sweater

GAUGE INFORMATION

13 sc and 15 rows = 3" (7.5 cm)
Gauge Swatch: 3" (7.5 cm) square
Ch 14.
Row 1: Sc in second ch from hook
and in each ch across.
Rows 2-15: Ch 1, turn; sc in each sc
across.
Finish off.

——STITCH GUIDE——

SINGLE CROCHET 2 TOGETHER
(abbreviated sc2tog)
Pull up a loop in each of next 2 sts, YO
and draw through all 3 loops on hook
(counts as one sc).

DOUBLE CROCHET 2 TOGETHER
(abbreviated dc2tog)
(uses next 2 sts)
★ YO, insert hook in **next** st, YO and
pull up a loop, YO and draw through
2 loops on hook; repeat from ★
once **more**, YO and draw through all
3 loops on hook **(counts as one dc)**.

SWEATER
YOKE

With Green, ch 54.

Row 1 (Right side)**:** Sc in second ch
from hook and in each ch across:
53 sc.

Note: Loop a short piece of yarn
around any stitch to mark Row 1 as
right side.

Row 2: Ch 1, turn; sc in first 7 sc, 3 sc
in next sc, sc in next 9 sc, 3 sc in next
sc, sc in next 17 sc, 3 sc in next sc, sc
in next 9 sc, 3 sc in next sc, sc in last
7 sc: 61 sc.

Rows 3-12: Ch 1, turn; ★ sc in each sc
across to center sc of next 3-sc group,
3 sc in center sc; repeat from ★ 3 times
more, sc in each sc across: 141 sc.

Finish off.

Row 13: With **wrong** side facing, join
White with slip st in first sc; (dc in next
sc, slip st in next sc) across; finish off.

BODY

With Green, ch 83; place marker
in third ch from hook for joining
placement.

Row 1 (Right side)**:** Dc in back
ridge of fourth ch from hook *(Fig. 2,
page 30)* and each ch across; finish off:
81 sts.

Note: Mark Row 1 as **right** side.

Row 2: With **wrong** side facing,
join White with slip st in first dc; (dc
in next dc, slip st in next st) across;
finish off.

Row 3: With **right** side facing, join
Green with slip st in first slip st;
ch 3 **(counts as first dc, now and
throughout)**, dc in next dc and in
each st across; finish off.

Rows 4-15: Repeat Rows 2 and 3,
6 times.

BOTTOM BAND

Foundation Row: With **right** side of
Row 15 facing, join White with
sc in first dc *(see Joining With Sc,
page 30)*; sc in next dc and in each dc
across.

Row 1: Ch 7, sc in back ridge of
second ch from hook and each ch
across, skip first sc on Foundation
Row, slip st in next 2 sc.

Row 2: Ch 1, turn; skip first 2 slip sts,
sc in Back Loop Only of each sc
across *(Fig. 1, page 30)*.

Row 3: Ch 1, turn; sc in Back Loop Only of each sc across, slip st in **both** loops of next 2 sc on Foundation Row.

Rows 4-80: Repeat Rows 2 and 3, 38 times; then repeat Row 2 once **more**.

Finish off.

ASSEMBLY
With Green, working across Row 13 on Yoke and in free loops of beginning ch on Body *(Fig. 3c, page 31)*, and beginning in marked ch, whipstitch first 19 sts together *(Fig. A, page 14)*; skip next 31 sts on Yoke and next ch on Body (armhole), whipstitch next 41 sts together; skip next 31 sts on Yoke and next ch on Body (armhole), whipstitch remaining 19 sts together.

SLEEVE
Rnd 1: With **right** side facing, join Green with slip st in free loop of skipped ch on Body; ch 2, working in skipped sts on Yoke, YO, insert hook in same slip st on Yoke as whipstitched into during assembly, YO and pull up a loop, YO and draw through 2 loops on hook, YO, insert hook in first dc skipped on Yoke, YO and pull up a loop, YO and draw through 2 loops on hook, YO and draw through all 3 loops on hook, dc in next 30 sts, YO, insert hook in same slip st on Yoke as whipstitched into during assembly, YO and pull up a loop, YO and draw through 2 loops on hook, YO, insert hook in same ch as joining (at underarm), YO and pull up a loop, YO and draw through 2 loops on hook, YO and draw through all 3 loops on hook, skip beginning ch-2; join with slip st

to first st, place loop from hook onto safety pin to keep piece from unraveling as you work the next rnd: 32 sts.

Hold safety pin and dropped yarn on **wrong** side, **now and throughout.**

Rnd 2: With **wrong** side facing, join White with slip st in same st as joining; dc in next st, (slip st in next st, dc in next st) around; join with slip st to first slip st, place loop from hook onto safety pin to keep piece from unraveling as you work the next rnd.

Rnd 3: With **right** side facing, insert hook in same st as joining, remove safety pin from Green and place loop onto hook, draw loop through st; ch 3, dc in next dc and in each st around; join with slip st to first dc, place loop from hook onto safety pin to keep piece from unraveling as you work the next rnd.

Rnd 4: With **wrong** side facing, remove safety pin from White and place loop onto hook; ch 2, slip st in same st as joining, dc in next dc, (slip st in next dc, dc in next dc) around; join with slip st to first slip st, place loop from hook onto safety pin to keep piece from unraveling as you work the next rnd.

Rnds 5-14: Repeat Rnds 3 and 4, 5 times.

Rnd 15: With **right** side facing, insert hook in same st as joining, remove safety pin from Green and place loop onto hook, draw loop through st; ch 3, dc in next dc and in each st around; join with slip st to first dc, finish off Green, do **not** cut White.

CUFF
Foundation Rnd: With **right** side facing and working **behind** Rnd 15, remove safety pin from White and place loop onto hook; ch 2, sc in same st as joining and in next dc, sc2tog, (sc in next 2 dc, sc2tog) around; join with slip st to first sc: 24 sc.

Begin working in rows.

Row 1: Ch 4, sc in second ch from hook and in each ch across, slip st in first 2 sc on Foundation Rnd.

Row 2: Ch 1, turn; skip first 2 slip sts, sc in Back Loop Only of each sc across.

Row 3: Ch 1, turn; sc in Back Loop Only of each sc across, slip st in **both** loops of next 2 sc on Foundation Rnd.

Rows 4-24: Repeat Rows 2 and 3, 10 times; then repeat Row 2 once **more**.

Finish off, leaving a long end for sewing.

Working in Front Loops Only on Row 24 *(Fig. 1, page 30)* and in free loop of chs on Row 1 *(Fig. 3b, page 31)*, whipstitch Cuff together.

Repeat for second Sleeve.

NECK BAND

Foundation Row: With **right** side facing and working in free loops of beginning ch on Yoke, join White with sc in first ch; sc in next 5 chs, pull up a loop in each of next 3 chs, YO and draw through all 4 loops on hook, sc in next 7 chs, pull up a loop in each of next 3 chs, YO and draw through all 4 loops on hook, sc in next 15 chs, pull up a loop in each of next 3 chs, YO and draw through all 4 loops on hook, sc in next 7 chs, pull up a loop in each of next 3 chs, YO and draw through all 4 loops on hook, sc in last 6 chs: 45 sts.

Row 1: Ch 4, sc in back ridge of second ch from hook and each ch across, skip first sc on Foundation Row, slip st in next 2 sc.

Row 2: Ch 1, turn; skip first 2 slip sts, sc in Back Loop Only of each sc across.

Row 3: Ch 1, turn; sc in Back Loop Only of each sc across, slip st in **both** loops of next 2 sts on Foundation Row.

Rows 4-44: Repeat Rows 2 and 3, 20 times; then repeat Row 2 once **more**.

Finish off.

RIGHT FRONT BAND

Row 1: With **right** side facing, working in free loops of chs on Row 1 of Bottom Band and Neck Band, and across end of rows on Body and Yoke, join White with sc in ch at base of first sc on Bottom Band; sc in next 5 chs and in next row, 2 sc in next row, skip next row, 2 sc in next row, (sc in next row, 2 sc in next row) 3 times, skip next row, 2 sc in next row, (sc in next row, 2 sc in next row) twice, sc in next 4 rows, skip next row, sc in next 3 rows, skip next row, sc in next 5 rows and in last 3 chs: 43 sc.

Row 2 (Buttonhole row): Ch 1, turn; sc in first 2 sc, ch 2, skip next 2 sc, ★ sc in next 7 sc, ch 2, skip next 2 sc; repeat from ★ 3 times **more**, sc in last 3 sc.

Row 3: Ch 1, turn; sc in each sc and in each ch across; finish off.

LEFT FRONT BAND

Row 1: With **right** side facing, working in sts on last row of Neck Band and Bottom Band and across end of rows on Yoke and Body, join White with sc in first sc on Neck Band; sc in next 2 sc and in next 5 rows, skip next row, sc in next 3 rows, skip next row, sc in next 4 rows, 2 sc in next row, (sc in next row, 2 sc in next row) twice, skip next row, 2 sc in next row, (sc in next row, 2 sc in next row) 3 times, skip next row, 2 sc in next row, sc in next row and in last 6 sc: 43 sc.

Rows 2 and 3: Ch 1, turn; sc in each sc across.

Finish off.

Sew buttons to Left Front Band opposite buttonholes.

CAP

Rnd 1 (Right side): With Green, ch 4, 11 dc in fourth ch from hook; join with slip st to top of beginning ch-4, ▦ place loop from hook onto safety pin to keep piece from unraveling as you work the next rnd: 12 sts.

Note: Loop a short piece of yarn around any stitch to mark Rnd 1 as **right** side.

Hold safety pin and dropped yarn on **wrong** side, now and throughout.

Rnd 2: With **wrong** side facing, join White with slip st in same st as joining; dc in next dc, (slip st in next dc, dc in next dc) around; join with slip st to first slip st, place loop from hook onto safety pin to keep piece from unraveling as you work the next rnd.

Rnd 3: With **right** side facing, insert hook in same st as joining, remove safety pin from Green and place loop onto hook, draw loop through st; ch 3 (**counts as first dc, now and throughout**), dc in same st, 2 dc in next dc and in each st around; join with slip st to first dc, place loop from hook onto safety pin to keep piece from unraveling as you work the next rnd: 24 dc.

Rnd 4: With **wrong** side facing, remove safety pin from White and place loop onto hook; ch 2, slip st in same st as joining, dc in next dc, (slip st in next dc, dc in next dc) around; join with slip st to first slip st, place loop from hook onto safety pin to keep piece from unraveling as you work the next rnd.

Rnds 5 and 6: Repeat Rnds 3 and 4: 48 sts.

Rnd 7: With **right** side facing, insert hook in same st as joining, remove safety pin from Green and place loop onto hook, draw loop through st; ch 3, dc in next 2 sts, 2 dc in next st, (dc in next 3 sts, 2 dc in next st) around; join with slip st to first dc, place loop from hook onto safety pin to keep piece from unraveling as you work the next rnd: 60 dc.

Rnd 8: With **wrong** side facing, remove safety pin from White and place loop onto hook; ch 2, slip st in same st as joining, dc in next dc, (slip st in next dc, dc in next dc) around; join with slip st to first slip st, place loop from hook onto safety pin to keep piece from unraveling as you work the next rnd.

Rnd 9: With **right** side facing, insert hook in same st as joining, remove safety pin from Green and place loop onto hook, draw loop through st; ch 3, dc in next dc and in each st around; join with slip st to first dc, place loop from hook onto safety pin to keep piece from unraveling as you work the next rnd.

Rnds 10-14: Repeat Rnds 8 and 9 twice, then repeat Rnd 8 once **more**.

Rnd 15: With **right** side facing, insert hook in same st as joining, remove safety pin from Green and place loop onto hook, draw loop through st; ch 3, dc in next dc and in each st around; join with slip st to first dc, finish off Green, do **not** cut White.

RIBBING

Foundation Rnd: With **right** side facing and working **behind** last rnd, remove safety pin from White and place loop onto hook; ch 2, sc in same st as joining and in each dc around; join with slip st to first sc: 60 sc.

Begin working in rows.

Row 1: Ch 9, sc in second ch from hook and in each ch across, slip st in first 2 sc on Foundation Rnd.

Row 2: Ch 1, turn; skip first 2 slip sts, sc in Back Loop Only of each sc across *(Fig. 1, page 30)*.

Row 3: Ch 1, turn; sc in Back Loop Only of each sc across, slip st in **both** loops of next 2 sc on Foundation Rnd.

Rows 4-60: Repeat Rows 2 and 3, 28 times; then repeat Row 2 once **more**.

Finish off, leaving a long end for sewing.

Working in Front Loops Only on Row 60 *(Fig.1, page 30)* and in free loop of chs on Row 1 *(Fig. 3b, page 31)*, whipstitch Ribbing together *(Fig. A, page 14)*.

With White, make a pom-pom *(Figs. 5a-c, page 31)* and sew to top of Cap.

BOOTIES
SOLE

With Green, ch 10.

Rnd 1 (Right side)**:** 3 Sc in second ch from hook, sc in next 7 chs, 5 sc in last ch; working in free loops of beginning ch *(Fig. 3b, page 31)*, sc in next 7 chs, 2 sc in same ch as first sc; join with slip st to first sc: 24 sc.

Note: Loop a short piece of yarn around any stitch to mark Rnd 1 as **right** side.

Rnd 2: Ch 1, 2 sc in same st, sc in next sc, 2 sc in next sc, sc in next 7 sc, 2 sc in next sc, (sc in next sc, 2 sc in next sc) twice, sc in next 7 sc, 2 sc in next sc, sc in last sc; join with slip st to first sc: 30 sc.

Rnd 3: Ch 1, sc in same st and in next sc, † 2 sc in next sc, sc in next sc, 2 sc in next sc, sc in next 7 sc, 2 sc in next sc, sc in next sc, 2 sc in next sc †, sc in next 2 sc, repeat from † to † once; join with slip st to first sc: 38 sc.

Rnd 4: Ch 1, sc in same st and in each sc around; join with slip st to Back Loop Only of first sc *(Fig. 1, page 30)*, do **not** finish off.

SIDES AND INSTEP

Rnd 1: Ch 3 **(counts as first dc, now and throughout)**, dc in Back Loop Only of next sc and each sc around; join with slip st to first dc, place loop from hook onto safety pin to keep piece from unraveling as you work the next rnd.

Hold safety pin and dropped yarn on **wrong** side, now and throughout.

Rnd 2: With **wrong** side facing, join White with slip st in same st as joining; working in both loops, dc in next dc, (slip st in next dc, dc in next dc) around; join with slip st to first slip st, place loop from hook onto safety pin to keep piece from unraveling as you work the next rnd.

Rnd 3: With **right** side facing, insert hook in same st as joining, remove safety pin from Green and place loop onto hook, draw loop through st; ch 3, dc in next 8 sts, dc2tog 10 times, dc in last 9 sts; join with slip st to first dc, place loop from hook onto safety pin to keep piece from unraveling as you work the next rnd: 28 dc.

Rnd 4: With **wrong** side facing, remove safety pin from White and place loop onto hook; ch 2, slip st in same st as joining, dc in next dc, (slip st in next dc, dc in next dc) around; join with slip st to first slip st, place loop from hook onto safety pin to keep piece from unraveling as you work the next rnd.

Rnd 5: With **right** side facing, insert hook in same st as joining, remove safety pin from Green and place loop onto hook, draw loop through st; ch 3, dc in next 10 sts, dc2tog 4 times, dc in last 9 sts; join with slip st to first dc, finish off Green, do **not** cut White: 24 dc.

CUFF

Foundation Rnd: With **right** side facing and working **behind** last rnd, remove safety pin from White and place loop onto hook; ch 2, sc in same st as joining and in each dc around; join with slip st to first sc.

Begin working in rows.

Row 1: Ch 8, sc in second ch from hook and in each ch across, slip st in first 2 sc on Foundation Rnd.

Row 2: Ch 1, turn; skip first 2 slip sts, sc in Back Loop Only of each sc across.

Row 3: Ch 1, turn; sc in Back Loop Only of each sc across, slip st in **both** loops of next 2 sc on Foundation Rnd.

Rows 4-24: Repeat Rows 2 and 3, 10 times; then repeat Row 2 once **more**.

Finish off, leaving a long end for sewing.

Working in ▦ Front Loops Only on Row 24 *(Fig. 1, page 30)* and in free loop of chs on Row 1, ▦ whipstitch *(Fig. A, page 14)* Cuff together.

AFGHAN

Finished Size: 34" x 45"
(86.5 cm x 114.5 m)

Each row is worked across length of Afghan Body. When joining yarn and finishing off White only, leave an 8" (20.5 cm) end to be worked into fringe.

AFGHAN BODY

With Green, ch 199, place marker in third ch from hook for st placement.

Row 1 (Right side): Dc in fourth ch from hook **(3 skipped chs count as first dc)** and in each ch across: 197 dc.

Note: Loop a short piece of yarn around any stitch to mark Row 1 as **right** side.

Row 2: Ch 3 **(counts as first dc, now and throughout)**, turn; dc in next dc and in each dc across; 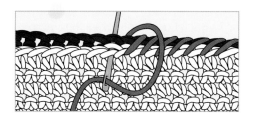 place loop onto safety pin to keep piece from unraveling as you work the next row.

Row 3: With **wrong** side facing, join White with slip st in first dc; (dc in next dc, slip st in next dc) across; finish off.

Row 4: With **right** side facing, insert hook in first slip st, remove safety pin and place loop onto hook, draw loop through st; ch 3, dc in next dc and in each st across.

Row 5: Ch 3, turn; dc in next dc and in each dc across; place loop onto safety pin to keep piece from unraveling as you work the next row.

Repeat Rows 3-5 until Afghan Body measures approximately 33" (84 cm) from beginning ch, ending by working Row 4.

Next Row: Ch 3, turn; dc in next dc and in each dc across; finish off.

Last Row: With **wrong** side facing, join White with slip st in first dc; (dc in next dc, slip st in next dc) across; finish off.

Trim: With **wrong** side facing and working in free loops of beginning ch *(Fig. 3b, page 31)*, join White with slip st in marked ch; (dc in next ch, slip st in next ch) across; finish off.

WHIPSTITCH

With **wrong** sides together, sew through both pieces once to secure the beginning of the seam, leaving an ample yarn end to weave in later. Working through **both** loops of each stitch on **both** pieces, insert the needle from **front** to **back** through first stitch and pull yarn through *(Fig. A)*, ★ insert the needle from **front** to **back** through next stitch and pull yarn through; repeat from ★ across.

Fig. A

FRINGE

Cut a piece of cardboard 3" x 9" (7.5 cm x 23 cm). Wind the yarn **loosely** and **evenly** lengthwise around the cardboard until the card is filled, then cut across one end; repeat as needed.

Using photo, page 13, as a guide for placement, add additional fringe across short edges of Afghan as follows:

Hold together 5 strands of yarn; fold in half.

With **wrong** side facing and using a crochet hook, draw the folded end up through a row and pull the loose ends through the folded end *(Fig. B)*; draw the knot up tightly *(Fig. C)*.

Lay flat on a hard surface and trim the ends.

Fig. B

Fig. C

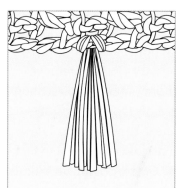

SHOPPING LIST

Yarn (Sport Weight)

[5 ounces, 459 yards
(141 grams, 420 meters)
per skein]:

☐ 7 skeins

Crochet Hook

☐ Size F (3.75 mm)
or size needed for gauge

Additional Supplies

☐ Yarn needle

☐ Sewing needle and thread

☐ ⅜" (10 mm) Buttons - 3 for
Sacque

☐ ¼"w (7 mm) Ribbon - 24"
(61 cm) for Bonnet

GAUGE INFORMATION

13 sc and 15 rows = 3" (7.5 cm)
In pattern,
(sc, ch 2, dc) 5 times = 3" (7.5 cm)
Gauge Swatch: 3" (7.5 cm) square
Ch 14.
Row 1: Sc in second ch from hook
and in each ch across.
Rows 2-15: Ch 1, turn; sc in each sc
across.
Finish off.

——STITCH GUIDE——

🎥 FRONT POST DOUBLE CROCHET
(abbreviated FPdc)

YO, insert hook from **front** to **back**
around post of st indicated *(Fig. 4,
page 31)*, YO and pull up a loop
(3 loops on hook), (YO and draw
through 2 loops on hook) twice. Skip
st **behind** FPdc.

🎥 BACK POST DOUBLE CROCHET
(abbreviated BPdc)

YO, insert hook from **back** to **front**
around post of st indicated *(Fig. 4,
page 31)*, YO and pull up a loop
(3 loops on hook), (YO and draw
through 2 loops on hook) twice.
Skip st in **front** of BPdc.

🎥 SINGLE CROCHET 2 TOGETHER
(abbreviated sc2tog)

Pull up a loop in each of next 2 sts, YO
and draw through all 3 loops on hook
(counts as one sc).

🎥 ADDING ON SINGLE CROCHETS

When instructed to add on sc at the
end of a row, insert hook into base
of last sc *(Fig. A)*, YO and pull up a
loop, YO and draw through one loop
on hook, YO and draw through both
loops on hook. Repeat as many times
as instructed.

Fig. A

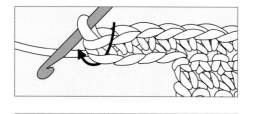

SACQUE

YOKE
BACK
Ch 40.

Row 1 (Right side): Sc in 🎥 back
ridge of second ch from hook and
each ch across *(Fig. 2, page 30)*: 39 sc.

Note: Loop a short piece of yarn
around any stitch to mark Row 1 as
right side.

Row 2: Ch 1, turn; sc in each sc across.

Row 3: Ch 1, turn; sc in first sc, work
FPdc around sc one row **below**
next sc, ★ sc in next 3 sc, work FPdc
around st one row **below** next sc;
repeat from ★ across to last sc, sc in
last sc.

Row 4: Ch 1, turn; sc in each st across.

Row 5: Ch 1, turn; sc in first sc, work
FPdc around FPdc one row **below**
next sc, ★ sc in next 3 sc, work FPdc
around FPdc one row **below** next sc;
repeat from ★ across to last sc, sc in
last sc.

Rows 6-15: Repeat Rows 4 and 5,
5 times.

LEFT SHOULDER
Row 1: Ch 1, turn; sc in first 11 sts,
leave remaining 28 sts unworked:
11 sc.

Row 2: Ch 1, turn; sc in first sc, work FPdc around FPdc one row **below** next sc, ★ sc in next 3 sc, work FPdc around FPdc one row **below** next sc; repeat from ★ once **more**, sc in last sc.

Row 3: Ch 1, turn; sc in each st across.

Rows 4-11: Repeat Rows 2 and 3, 4 times; do **not** finish off.

LEFT FRONT

Row 1: Ch 9, turn; sc in back ridge of second ch from hook and next 7 chs, sc in next sc, work FPdc around FPdc one row **below** next sc, ★ sc in next 3 sc, work FPdc around FPdc one row **below** next sc; repeat from ★ once **more**, sc in last sc: 19 sts.

Row 2: Ch 1, turn; sc in each st across.

Row 3: Ch 1, turn; sc in first sc, work FPdc around sc one row **below** next sc, ★ sc in next 3 sc, work FPdc around st one row **below** next sc; repeat from ★ across to last sc, sc in last sc.

Row 4: Ch 1, turn; sc in each st across.

Row 5: Ch 1, turn; sc in first sc, work FPdc around FPdc one row **below** next sc, ★ sc in next 3 sc, work FPdc around FPdc one row **below** next sc; repeat from ★ across to last sc, sc in last sc.

Rows 6-15: Repeat Rows 4 and 5, 5 times.

Finish off.

RIGHT SHOULDER

Row 1: With **wrong** side facing, skip next 17 sts on Row 15 of Back from Left Shoulder and ▦ join yarn with sc in next sc *(see Joining With Sc, page 30)*; sc in each st across: 11 sc.

Row 2: Ch 1, turn; sc in first sc, work FPdc around FPdc one row **below** next sc, ★ sc in next 3 sc, work FPdc around FPdc one row **below** next sc; repeat from ★ once **more**, sc in last sc.

Row 3: Ch 1, turn; sc in each st across.

Rows 4-11: Repeat Rows 2 and 3, 4 times; do **not** finish off.

RIGHT FRONT

Row 1: Ch 1, turn; sc in first sc, work FPdc around FPdc one row **below** next sc, ★ sc in next 3 sc, work FPdc around FPdc one row **below** next sc; repeat from ★ once **more**, sc in next sc, add on 8 sc *(Fig. A, page 16)*: 19 sts.

Row 2: Ch 1, turn; sc in each st across.

Row 3: Ch 1, turn; sc in first sc, work FPdc around FPdc one row **below** next sc, ★ sc in next 3 sc, work FPdc around st one row **below** next sc; repeat from ★ across to last sc, sc in last sc.

Row 4: Ch 1, turn; sc in each st across.

Row 5: Ch 1, turn; sc in first sc, work FPdc around FPdc one row **below** next sc, ★ sc in next 3 sc, work FPdc around FPdc one row **below** next sc; repeat from ★ across to last sc, sc in last sc.

Rows 6-15: Repeat Rows 4 and 5, 5 times.

Finish off.

BODY

Row 1: With **right** side facing, join yarn with sc in first sc on Row 15 of Left Front; sc in next 18 sts, ch 1; working in ▦ free loops of beginning ch across Back *(Fig. 3c, page 31)*, sc in next 39 sts, ch 1; working across Row 15 of Right Front, sc in last 19 sts: 77 sc and 2 chs.

Row 2: Ch 1, turn; working in ▦ Front Loops Only *(Fig. 1, page 30)*, (sc, ch 2, dc) in first sc, ★ skip next sc or ch, (sc, ch 2, dc) in next sc; repeat from ★ across to last 2 sc, skip next sc, sc in last sc: 39 ch-2 sps.

Row 3: Ch 3 (**counts as first dc, now and throughout**), turn; working in both loops, dc in same st, (sc, ch 2, dc) in each ch-2 sp across to last ch-2 sp, sc in last ch-2 sp, ch 2, dc in last sc.

Row 4: Ch 1, turn; sc in first dc, ch 2, dc in next ch-2 sp, (sc, ch 2, dc) in each ch-2 sp across, skip next 2 sts, sc in last dc.

Row 5: Ch 3, turn; dc in same st, (sc, ch 2, dc) in each ch-2 sp across to last ch-2 sp, sc in last ch-2 sp, ch 2, dc in last sc.

Rows 6-18: Repeat Rows 4 and 5, 6 times; then repeat Row 4 once **more**.

Row 19: Ch 3, turn; dc in same st, (sc, ch 2, dc) in each ch-2 sp across to last ch-2 sp, sc in last ch-2 sp, ch 2, slip st in last sc; finish off.

SLEEVE

Rnd 1: With **right** side facing, join yarn with sc in ch at underarm; work 25 sc evenly spaced across end of rows on Yoke; join with slip st to first sc: 26 sc.

Rnd 2: Ch 1, turn; (sc, ch 2, dc) in same st, skip next sc, ★ (sc, ch 2, dc) in next sc, skip next sc; repeat from ★ around; join with slip st to first sc: 13 ch-2 sps.

Rnd 3: Ch 3, turn; dc in same st, (sc, ch 2, dc) in each ch-2 sp around to last ch-2 sp, sc in last ch-2 sp, ch 2; join with slip st to first dc.

Rnd 4: Ch 1, turn; sc in same st, ch 2, dc in next ch-2 sp, (sc, ch 2, dc) in each ch-2 sp around; join with slip st to first sc.

Rnds 5-12: Repeat Rnds 3 and 4, 4 times; do **not** finish off.

CUFF

Rnd 1: Ch 1, turn; work 20 sc evenly spaced around; join with slip st to Back Loop Only of first sc *(Fig. 1, page 30)*.

Rnd 2: Ch 1, do **not** turn; sc in Back Loop Only of same st and each sc around; join with slip st to **both** loops of first sc.

Rnd 3: Ch 1, **turn**; sc in both loops of same st and each sc around; join with slip st to first sc.

Rnd 4: Ch 1, turn; sc in same st and in next sc, work FPdc around sc one rnd **below** next sc, ★ sc in next 3 sc, work FPdc around sc one rnd **below** next sc; repeat from ★ around to last sc, sc in last sc; join with slip st to first sc.

Rnd 5: Ch 1, turn; sc in same st and in each sc around; join with slip st to first sc.

Rnd 6: Ch 1, turn; sc in same st and in next sc, work FPdc around FPdc one rnd **below** next sc, ★ sc in next 3 sc, work FPdc around FPdc one rnd **below** next sc; repeat from ★ around to last sc, sc in last sc; join with slip st to first sc.

Rnds 7 and 8: Repeat Rnds 5 and 6.

Finish off.

SLEEVE TRIM

With **right** side facing and working in free loops of sc on Rnd 1 of Cuff *(Fig. 3a, page 31)*, join yarn with slip st in any st; ch 1, (slip st in next sc, ch 1) around; join with slip st to first slip st, finish off.

Repeat for second Sleeve.

NECK BAND

Row 1: With **right** side facing, join yarn with sc in st at base of first sc on Right Front neck; sc in next 6 sts; work 8 sc evenly spaced across end of rows on Right Shoulder; sc in next 17 sts on Back; work 8 sc evenly spaced across end of rows on Left Shoulder; working in free loop of chs across Left Front neck, skip next ch, sc in last 7 chs: 47 sc.

Row 2: Ch 1, turn; sc in Front Loop Only of each sc across.

Row 3: Ch 1, turn; sc in both loops of each sc across.

Row 4: Ch 1, turn; sc in first sc, work BPdc around sc one row **below** next sc, ★ sc in next 3 sc, work BPdc around sc one row **below** next sc; repeat from ★ across to last sc, sc in last sc.

Row 5: Ch 1, turn; sc in each st across.

Row 6: Ch 1, turn; sc in first sc, work BPdc around BPdc one row **below** next sc, ★ sc in next 3 sc, work BPdc around BPdc one row **below** next sc; repeat from ★ across to last sc, sc in last sc; do **not** finish off.

TRIM

Turn; slip st in each st across; working in end of rows across Neck Band and Left Front, 2 sc in first row, sc in next 2 rows, skip next row, (sc in next 6 rows, skip next row) twice, sc in next 2 rows, ch 1; working in free loops of sc and chs and in Front Loops Only of skipped sc on Row 1 of Body, slip st in first sc, ch 1, (slip st in next st, ch 1) across; working in end of rows across Right Front, sc in first row, ch 4, slip st in top of sc just made (buttonhole made), sc in next row, skip next row, ★ sc in next 5 rows, ch 4, slip st in top of sc just made, sc in next row, skip next row; repeat from ★ once **more**, sc in next 2 rows, 2 sc in last row; join with slip st to first slip st, finish off.

NECK TRIM

With **right** side facing, top edge of Neck Band toward you, and working in free loops of sc on Row 1 of Neck Band, join yarn with sc in first sc; ch 2, dc in same st, ★ skip next sc, (sc, ch 2, dc) in next sc; repeat from ★ across to last 2 sc, skip next sc, sc in last sc; finish off.

Sew buttons to Left Front Band opposite buttonholes.

BONNET
BACK
Ch 12.

Row 1: Sc in second ch from hook and in each ch across: 11 sc.

Row 2 (Right side): Ch 1, turn; 2 sc in first sc, sc in each sc across to last sc, 2 sc in last sc: 13 sc.

Note: Loop a short piece of yarn around any stitch to mark Row 2 as **right** side.

Rows 3 and 4: Ch 1, turn; sc in each sc across.

Row 5: Ch 1, turn; 2 sc in first sc, sc in each sc across to last sc, 2 sc in last sc: 15 sc.

Rows 6-8: Repeat Rows 3-5: 17 sc.

Rows 9-11: Ch 1, turn; sc in each sc across.

Row 12: Ch 1, turn; 2 sc in first sc, sc in each sc across to last sc, 2 sc in last sc: 19 sc.

Rows 13-16: Repeat Rows 9-12: 21 sc.

Rows 17-25: Ch 1, turn; sc in each sc across.

Rows 26-31: Ch 1, turn; skip first sc, sc in next sc and in each sc across to last 2 sc, sc2tog: 9 sc.

Finish off.

CROWN
Row 1: With **right** side facing, 🎥 join yarn with sc in end of Row 1 *(see Joining With Sc, page 30)*; work 24 sc 🎥 evenly spaced across end of rows; sc in each sc across Row 31; work 25 sc evenly spaced across end of rows to Row 1: 59 sc.

Row 2: Ch 1, turn; sc in 🎥 Front Loop Only of each sc across *(Fig. 1, page 30)*.

Row 3: Ch 1, turn; sc in both loops of each sc across.

Row 4: Ch 1, turn; sc in first sc, work BPdc around sc one row **below** next sc, ★ sc in next 3 sc, work BPdc around sc one row **below** next sc; repeat from ★ across to last sc, sc in last sc.

Row 5: Ch 1, turn; sc in each st across.

Row 6: Ch 1, turn; sc in first sc, work BPdc around BPdc one row **below** next sc, ★ sc in next 3 sc, work BPdc around BPdc one row **below** next sc; repeat from ★ across to last sc, sc in last sc.

Row 7: Ch 1, turn; sc in each st across.

Rows 8-19: Repeat Rows 6 and 7, 6 times.

Row 20: Ch 1, turn; working in Front Loops Only, (sc, ch 2, dc) in first sc, ★ skip next sc, (sc, ch 2, dc) in next sc; repeat from ★ across to last 2 sc, skip next sc, sc in last sc.

Row 21: Ch 3, turn; dc in same st, (sc, ch 2, dc) in each ch-2 sp across to last ch-2 sp, sc in last ch-2 sp, ch 2, dc in last sc; finish off.

FRONT TRIM
With **right** side facing, Back toward you, and working in sc across Row 19 of Crown, join yarn with slip st in 🎥 free loop of first sc *(Fig. 3a, page 31)*; ★ ch 1, slip st in Front Loop Only of next sc, ch 1, slip st in free loop of next sc; repeat from ★ across; do **not** finish off.

NECK EDGING
Ch 1; working in end of rows on Crown and in 🎥 free loops of beginning ch on Back *(Fig. 3b, page 31)*, sc in Row 18, skip next row, sc in next row, (skip next row, sc in next 2 rows) 4 times, skip next row, pull up a loop in next row, skip next row, pull up a loop in first ch on Back, YO and draw through all 3 loops on hook, sc2tog twice, sc in next ch, sc2tog twice, pull up a loop in last ch, skip first row on Crown, pull up a loop in next row, YO and draw through all 3 loops on hook, (skip next row, sc in next 2 rows) 4 times, (skip next row, sc in next row) twice, ch 1; join with slip st to joining slip st on Front Trim, finish off.

Sew a 12" (30.5 cm) length of ribbon to each corner of Neck Edging for tie.

BOOTIES
SOLE
Ch 10.

Rnd 1 (Right side): 3 Sc in second ch from hook, sc in next 7 chs, 5 sc in last ch; working in 🎥 free loops of beginning ch *(Fig. 3b, page 31)*, sc in next 7 chs, 2 sc in same ch as first sc; join with slip st to first sc: 24 sc.

Note: Loop a short piece of yarn around any stitch to mark Rnd 1 as **right** side.

Rnd 2: Ch 1, 2 sc in same st, sc in next sc, 2 sc in next sc, sc in next 7 sc, 2 sc in next sc, (sc in next sc, 2 sc in next sc) twice, sc in next 7 sc, 2 sc in next sc, sc in last sc; join with slip st to first sc: 30 sc.

Rnd 3: Ch 1, sc in same st and in next sc, † 2 sc in next sc, sc in next sc, 2 sc in next sc, sc in next 7 sc, 2 sc in next sc, sc in next sc, 2 sc in next sc †, sc in next 2 sc, repeat from † to † once; join with slip st to first sc: 38 sc.

Rnd 4: Ch 1, sc in same st and in each sc around; join with slip st to 📽 Back Loop Only of first sc *(Fig. 1, page 30)*, do **not** finish off.

SIDES AND INSTEP

Rnd 1: Ch 1, sc in Back Loop Only of same st and each sc around; join with slip st to **both** loops of first sc.

Rnds 2-4: Ch 1, turn; sc in **both** loops of same st and each sc around; join with slip st to first sc.

Rnd 5: Ch 1, turn; sc in same st and in next 15 sc, sc2tog, sc in next sc, sc2tog twice, sc in next sc, sc2tog, sc in last 12 sc; join with slip st to first sc: 34 sc.

Rnd 6: Ch 1, turn; sc in same st and in next 11 sc, sc2tog, (sc in next sc, sc2tog) twice, sc in last 14 sc; join with slip st to first sc: 31 sc.

Rnd 7: Ch 1, turn; sc in same st and in next 13 sc, sc2tog, pull up a loop in each of next 3 sc, YO and draw through all 4 loops on hook, sc2tog, sc in last 10 sc; join with slip st to first sc: 27 sts.

Rnd 8: Ch 1, turn; sc in same st and in next 9 sc, sc2tog, pull up a loop in each of next 3 sts, YO and draw through all 4 loops on hook, sc2tog, sc in last 10 sc; join with slip st to first sc: 23 sts.

Rnd 9: Ch 1, turn; sc in same st and in next 9 sc, sc2tog 3 times, sc in last 7 sc; join with slip st to Back Loop Only of first sc, do **not** finish off: 20 sc.

CUFF

Rnd 1: Ch 1, do **not** turn; sc in Back Loop Only of same st and each sc around; join with slip st to **both** loops of first sc.

Rnd 2: Ch 1, turn; sc in both loops of same st and each st around; join with slip st to first sc.

Rnd 3: Ch 1, turn; sc in same st, work FPdc around st one rnd **below** next sc, ★ sc in next 3 sc, work FPdc around st one rnd **below** next sc; repeat from ★ around to last 2 sc, sc in last 2 sc; join with slip st to first sc.

Rnds 4-7: Repeat Rnds 2 and 3 twice.

Finish off.

TRIM

With **right** side facing, top of Cuff toward you, and working in 📽 free loops on Rnd 9 of Instep *(Fig. 3a, page 31)*, 📽 join yarn with sc in any sc *(see Joining With Sc, page 30)*; ch 2, dc in same st, skip next sc, ★ (sc, ch 2, dc) in next sc, skip next sc; repeat from ★ around; join with slip st to first sc, finish off.

AFGHAN

Finished Size: 36" x 48"
 (91.5 cm x 122 cm)

AFGHAN BODY

Ch 138.

Row 1 (Right side): Sc in second ch from hook and in each ch across: 137 sc.

Note: Loop a short piece of yarn around any stitch to mark Row 1 as **right** side.

Row 2: Ch 1, turn; sc in each sc across.

Row 3: Ch 1, turn; sc in first 2 sc, work FPdc around sc one row **below** next sc, ★ sc in next 3 sc, work FPdc around sc one row **below** next sc; repeat from ★ across to last 2 sc, sc in last 2 sc.

Row 4: Ch 1, turn; sc in each st across.

Row 5: Ch 1, turn; sc in first 2 sc, work FPdc around FPdc one row **below** next sc, ★ sc in next 3 sc, work FPdc around FPdc one row **below** next sc; repeat from ★ across to last 2 sc, sc in last 2 sc.

Repeat Rows 4 and 5 until Afghan Body measures approximately 43½" (110.5 cm) from beginning ch, ending by working Row 5; do **not** finish off.

BORDER

Rnd 1: Ch 1, do **not** turn; 2 sc in same st; work 189 sc evenly spaced across end of rows; working in free loops of beginning ch *(Fig. 3b, page 31)*, 3 sc in first ch, sc in each ch across to ch at base of last sc, 3 sc in ch at base of last sc; work 189 sc evenly spaced across end of rows; working across last row of Afghan Body, 3 sc in first sc, sc in each st across and in same st as first sc; join with slip st to Back Loop Only of first sc *(Fig. 1, page 30)*: 660 sc.

Rnd 2: Ch 1, working in Back Loops Only, (sc, ch 2, dc) in same st, skip next 2 sc, ★ † (sc, ch 2, dc) in next sc, skip next 2 sc †; repeat from † to † across to center sc of next corner 3-sc group, (sc, ch 2, dc) in center sc, place marker around ch-2 just made to mark corner, (sc, ch 2, dc) in same st, skip next 2 sc; repeat from ★ 2 times **more**, then repeat from † to † across, (sc, ch 2, dc) in same st as first sc; join with slip st to first sc: 224 ch-2-sps.

Rnd 3: Slip st in next ch-2 sp, ch 1, **turn**; (sc, ch 2, dc) in same sp and in next ch-2 sp, place marker around last ch-2 made to mark corner, (sc, ch 2, dc) in same sp, ★ (sc, ch 2, dc) in each ch-2 sp across to next marked corner ch-2 sp, (sc, ch 2, dc) in corner ch-2 sp, remove marker and place around ch-2 just made, (sc, ch 2, dc) in same sp; repeat from ★ 2 times **more**, (sc, ch 2, dc) in each ch-2 sp across; join with slip st to first sc: 228 ch-2 sps.

Rnd 4: Slip st in next ch-2 sp, ch 1, turn; ★ (sc, ch 2, dc) in same sp and in each ch-2 sp across to next marked corner ch-2 sp, (sc, ch 2, dc) in corner ch-2 sp, remove marker and place around ch-2 just made; repeat from ★ 3 times **more**, (sc, ch 2, dc) in same sp; join with slip st to first sc: 232 ch-2 sps.

Rnds 5-7: Repeat Rnds 3 and 4 once, then repeat Rnd 3 once **more**: 244 ch-2 sps.

Rnd 8: Slip st in next ch-2 sp, ch 1, turn; ★ (sc, ch 2, dc) in same sp and in each ch-2 sp across to next marked corner ch-2 sp, (sc, ch 2, dc) in corner ch-2 sp, remove marker; repeat from ★ 3 times **more**, (sc, ch 2, dc) in same sp; join with slip st to first sc, finish off.

TRIM

With **right** side facing and working in free loops of sc *(Fig. 3a, page 31)* and in Front Loops Only of skipped sc on Rnd 1 of Border *(Fig. 1, page 30)*, join yarn with slip st in any sc; ch 1, (slip st in next sc, ch 1) around; join with slip st to first slip st, finish off.

21

Blue Set

SHOPPING LIST

Yarn (Light Weight)

[1.75 ounces, 161 yards
(50 grams, 147 meters) per skein]:

☐ 17 skeins

Crochet Hook

☐ Size F (3.75 mm)
or size needed for gauge

Additional Supplies

☐ Yarn needle
☐ Sewing needle and thread
☐ ³⁄₈" (10 mm) Buttons - 3 for
Sacque
☐ ¼"w (7 mm) Ribbon - 36"
(91.5 cm) for Bonnet
☐ ¼"w (7 mm) Ribbon - 36"
(91.5 cm) for Booties
☐ ³⁄₈"w (10 mm) Ribbon -
5½ yards (5 meters) for Afghan

GAUGE INFORMATION

13 sc and 15 rows = 3" (7.5 cm)
In pattern,
2 repeats = 3¼" (8.25 cm)
Gauge Swatch: 3" (7.5 cm) square
Ch 14.
Row 1: Sc in second ch from hook
and in each ch across.
Rows 2-15: Ch 1, turn; sc in each sc
across.
Finish off.

—— STITCH GUIDE ——

🎥 **SINGLE CROCHET 2 TOGETHER**
(abbreviated sc2tog)
Pull up a loop in each of next 2 sts, YO
and draw through all 3 loops on hook
(counts as one sc).

🎥 **DOUBLE CROCHET 2 TOGETHER**
(abbreviated dc2tog)
(uses next 2 dc)
★ YO, insert hook in **next** dc, YO and
pull up a loop, YO and draw through
2 loops on hook; repeat from ★ once
more, YO and draw through all 3 loops
on hook.

SACQUE
YOKE

Ch 52.

Row 1: Sc in 🎥 back ridge of second
ch from hook and each ch across
(Fig. 2, page 30): 51 sc.

Row 2 (Right side)**:** Ch 1, turn; sc in
each sc across.

Note: Loop a short piece of yarn
around any stitch to mark Row 2 as
right side.

Row 3: Ch 1, turn; sc in first 2 sc, 2 sc in
next sc, (sc in next 2 sc, 2 sc in next sc)
across to last 3 sc, sc in last 3 sc: 67 sc.

Rows 4 and 5: Ch 1, turn; sc in each sc
across.

Row 6: Ch 1, turn; sc in first 3 sc, (2 sc
in next sc, sc in next 3 sc) across: 83 sc.

Rows 7 and 8: Ch 1, turn; sc in each sc
across.

Row 9: Ch 1, turn; sc in first 4 sc, 2 sc
in next sc, (sc in next 4 sc, 2 sc in next
sc) across to last 3 sc, sc in last 3 sc:
99 sc.

Rows 10 and 11: Ch 1, turn; sc in
each sc across.

Row 12: Ch 1, turn; sc in first 4 sc, 2 sc
in next sc, (sc in next 5 sc, 2 sc in next
sc) across to last 4 sc, sc in last 4 sc:
115 sc.

Rows 13 and 14: Ch 1, turn; sc in
each sc across.

Row 15: Ch 1, turn; sc in first 4 sc, 2 sc
in next sc, (sc in next 6 sc, 2 sc in next
sc) across to last 5 sc, sc in last 5 sc:
131 sc.

Rows 16 and 17: Ch 1, turn; sc in
each sc across.

Row 18: Ch 1, turn; sc in first 5 sc,
2 sc in next sc, (sc in next 16 sc, 2 sc
in next sc) across to last 6 sc, sc in last
6 sc; do **not** finish off: 139 sc.

BODY

Row 1: Ch 5 **(counts as first dc plus
ch 2, now and throughout)**, turn; skip
next sc, sc in next sc, skip next 2 sc,
(2 dc, ch 2, 2 dc) in next sc, skip next
2 sc, sc in next sc, ★ ch 3, skip next sc,
sc in next sc, skip next 2 sc, (2 dc, ch 2,
2 dc) in next sc, skip next 2 sc, sc in
next sc; repeat from ★ across to last
2 sc, ch 2, skip next sc, dc in last sc:
104 sts and 35 sps.

Row 2: Ch 1, turn; sc in first dc, † skip next sc, dc2tog, ch 4, sc in next ch-2 sp, ch 4, dc2tog, sc in next ch-3 sp †; repeat from † to † once **more**, place marker around same ch-3 just worked into, ch 7, skip next 7 sps, sc in next ch-3 sp (armhole), repeat from † to † 5 times, place marker around same ch-3 just worked into, ch 7, skip next 7 sps, sc in next ch-3 sp (armhole), repeat from † to † once, skip next sc, dc2tog, ch 4, sc in next ch-2 sp, ch 4, dc2tog, skip last ch-2 sp, sc in last dc: 39 sts, 18 ch-4 sps, and 2 ch-7 sps.

Row 3: Ch 4 (**counts as first dc plus ch 1, now and throughout**), turn; 2 dc in same st, † sc in next ch-4 sp, ch 3, sc in next ch-4 sp, skip next dc2tog, (2 dc, ch 2, 2 dc) in next sc †; repeat from † to † once **more**, skip next 2 chs, sc in next ch, ch 3, skip next ch, sc in next ch, (2 dc, ch 2, 2 dc) in next sc, repeat from † to † 5 times, skip next 2 chs, sc in next ch, ch 3, skip next ch, sc in next ch, [(2 dc, ch 2, 2 dc) in next sc, sc in next ch-4 sp, ch 3, sc in next ch-4 sp] twice, (2 dc, ch 1, dc) in last sc: 68 sts and 23 sps.

Row 4: Ch 1, turn; sc in first dc, ch 4, dc2tog, sc in next ch-3 sp, skip next sc, dc2tog, ch 4, ★ sc in next ch-2 sp, ch 4, dc2tog, sc in next ch-3 sp, skip next sc, dc2tog, ch 4; repeat from ★ across to last dc, sc in last dc: 45 sts and 22 ch-4 sps.

Row 5: Ch 5, turn; sc in next ch-4 sp, skip next dc2tog, (2 dc, ch 2, 2 dc) in next sc, sc in next ch-4 sp, ★ ch 3, sc in next ch-4 sp, skip next dc2tog, (2 dc, ch 2, 2 dc) in next sc, sc in next ch-4 sp; repeat from ★ across to last sc, ch 2, dc in last sc: 68 sts and 23 sps.

Row 6: Ch 1, turn; sc in first dc, skip next sc, dc2tog, ch 4, sc in next ch-2 sp, ch 4, dc2tog, ★ sc in next ch-3 sp, skip next sc, dc2tog, ch 4, sc in next ch-2 sp, ch 4, dc2tog; repeat from ★ across to last ch-2 sp, skip last ch-2 sp, sc in last dc: 45 sts and 22 ch-4 sps.

Row 7: Ch 4, turn; 2 dc in same st, sc in next ch-4 sp, ch 3, sc in next ch-4 sp, ★ skip next dc2tog, (2 dc, ch 2, 2 dc) in next sc, sc in next ch-4 sp, ch 3, sc in next ch-4 sp; repeat from ★ across to last 2 sts, skip next dc2tog, (2 dc, ch 1, dc) in last sc: 68 sts and 23 sps.

Rows 8-16: Repeat Rows 4-7 twice, then repeat Row 4 once **more**.

Finish off.

SLEEVE

Underarm Foundation Row: With **wrong** side of underarm facing, 📹 join yarn with sc in marked ch-3 sp (*see Joining With Sc, page 30*); ch 2, working in sps across underarm ch, sc in next ch-2 sp, (2 dc, ch 2, 2 dc) in next ch-1 sp, sc in next ch-2 sp, ch 2, sc in next ch-3 sp on Row 1 of Body, leave remaining sts unworked.

Begin working in rounds.

Rnd 1: Ch 1, **turn**; sc in first sc, skip next ch-2 sp and next sc, dc2tog, ch 4, sc in next ch-2 sp, ch 4, dc2tog, skip next sc, sc in next sc; working in skipped sts on Row 1 of Body, skip next sc, dc2tog, ch 4, sc in next ch-2 sp, ch 4, dc2tog, ★ sc in next ch-3 sp, skip next sc, dc2tog, ch 4, sc in next ch-2 sp, ch 4, dc2tog; repeat from ★ 2 times **more**; join with slip st to first sc: 10 ch-4 sps.

Rnd 2: Ch 3 (**counts as first dc**), turn; dc in same st, sc in next ch-4 sp, ch 3, sc in next ch-4 sp, skip next dc2tog, ★ (2 dc, ch 2, 2 dc) in next sc, sc in next ch-4 sp, ch 3, sc in next ch-4 sp, skip next dc2tog; repeat from ★ around, 2 dc in same st as first dc, ch 2; join with slip st to first dc.

Rnd 3: Ch 1, turn; sc in first ch-2 sp, ch 4, dc2tog, sc in next ch-3 sp, skip next sc, dc2tog, ★ ch 4, sc in next ch-2 sp, ch 4, dc2tog, sc in next ch-3 sp, skip next sc, dc2tog; repeat from ★ around, ch 2, hdc in first sc to form last ch-4 sp.

Rnd 4: Ch 1, turn; sc in last ch-4 sp made, skip next dc2tog, (2 dc, ch 2, 2 dc) in next sc, sc in next ch-4 sp, ★ ch 3, sc in next ch-4 sp, skip next dc2tog, (2 dc, ch 2, 2 dc) in next sc, sc in next ch-4 sp; repeat from ★ around, ch 2, sc in first sc to form last ch-3 sp.

Rnd 5: Ch 1, turn; sc in last ch-3 sp made, skip next sc, dc2tog, ch 4, sc in next ch-2 sp, ch 4, dc2tog, ★ sc in next ch-3 sp, skip next sc, dc2tog, ch 4, sc in next ch-2 sp, ch 4, dc2tog; repeat from ★ around; join with slip st to first sc.

Rnds 6-13: Repeat Rnds 2-5 twice; do **not** finish off.

CUFF

Rnd 1: Ch 1, do **not** turn; ★ sc in next dc2tog, 2 sc in each of next 2 ch-4 sps, sc in next dc2tog, skip next sc; repeat from ★ around; join with slip st to first sc: 30 sc.

Rnd 2: Ch 1, sc in same st, sc2tog, (sc in next sc, sc2tog) around; join with slip st to first sc: 20 sc.

Rnds 3 and 4: Ch 1, sc in same st and in each sc around; join with slip st to first sc.

Finish off.

Repeat for second Sleeve.

RIGHT FRONT BAND

Row 1: With **right** side facing and working in end of rows on Body and Yoke, join yarn with sc in Row 16 of Body; 2 sc in next row, (sc in next row, 2 sc in next row) 7 times, (sc in next 4 rows, skip next row) 3 times, sc in last 3 rows: 39 sc.

Row 2 (Buttonhole row)**:** Ch 1, turn; sc in first sc, ch 1, skip next sc, ★ sc in next 5 sc, ch 1, skip next sc; repeat from ★ once **more**, sc in each sc across: 36 sc and 3 ch-1 sps.

Row 3: Ch 1, turn; sc in each sc and in each ch across; finish off.

LEFT FRONT BAND

Row 1: With **right** side facing and working in end of rows on Yoke and Body, join yarn with sc in Row 1 of Yoke; sc in next 2 rows, (skip next row, sc in next 4 rows) 3 times, (2 sc in next row, sc in next row) across: 39 sc.

Row 2: Ch 1, turn; sc in each sc across.

Row 3: Ch 1, turn; sc in each sc across to last sc, 2 sc in last sc; do **not** finish off.

BOTTOM EDGING

Sc in end of next row and in next sc, ★ 3 sc in next ch-4 sp, sc in next dc2tog, skip next sc, sc in next dc2tog, 3 sc in next ch-4 sp, sc in next sc; repeat from ★ 10 times **more**, sc in next row and in same st as first sc on Row 3 of Right Front Band; join with slip st to first sc, finish off.

NECK TRIM

Row 1: With **wrong** side facing, working in end of rows on Front Bands and in ▥ free loops of beginning ch on Yoke *(Fig. 3c, page 31)*, join yarn with sc in end of Row 3 on Left Front Band; sc in next 2 rows, sc in next 51 chs and in last 3 rows: 57 sc.

Row 2: Ch 1, turn; sc in first sc, ★ skip next sc, 4 dc in next sc, skip next sc, sc in next sc; repeat from ★ across; finish off.

Sew buttons to Left Front Band opposite buttonholes.

BONNET
BACK

Ch 13.

Row 1: Sc in second ch from hook and in each ch across: 12 sc.

Rows 2 and 3: Ch 1, turn; sc in each sc across.

Row 4 (Right side)**:** Ch 1, turn; 2 sc in first sc, sc in each sc across to last sc, 2 sc in last sc: 14 sc.

Note: Loop a short piece of yarn around any stitch to mark Row 4 as **right** side.

Rows 5-7: Ch 1, turn; sc in each sc across.

Row 8: Ch 1, turn; 2 sc in first sc, sc in each sc across to last sc, 2 sc in last sc: 16 sc.

Rows 9-16: Repeat Rows 5-8 twice: 20 sc.

Rows 17-23: Ch 1, turn; sc in each sc across.

Rows 24 and 25: Ch 1, turn; pull up a loop in each of first 2 sc, YO and draw through all 3 loops on hook, sc in each sc across to last 2 sts, sc2tog: 16 sts.

Row 26: Ch 1, turn; sc in each st across.

Row 27: Ch 1, turn; pull up a loop in each of first 2 sc, YO and draw through all 3 loops on hook, sc in each sc across to last 2 sc, sc2tog: 14 sts.

Rows 28 and 29: Repeat Rows 26 and 27: 12 sts.

Row 30: Ch 1, turn; sc in each st across; finish off.

CROWN

Row 1: With **right** side facing, ▥ join yarn with sc in end of Row 1 *(see Joining With Sc, page 30)*; work 26 sc ▥ evenly spaced across end of rows; 2 sc in first sc on Row 30, sc in each sc across; work 27 sc evenly spaced across end of rows: 67 sc.

Row 2: Ch 5 (**counts as first dc plus ch 2, now and throughout**), turn; skip next sc, sc in next sc, skip next 2 sc, (2 dc, ch 2, 2 dc) in next sc, skip next 2 sc, sc in next sc, ★ ch 3, skip next sc, sc in next sc, skip next 2 sc, (2 dc, ch 2, 2 dc) in next sc, skip next 2 sc, sc in next sc; repeat from ★ across to last 2 sc, ch 2, skip next sc, dc in last sc: 50 sts and 17 sps.

Row 3: Ch 1, turn; sc in first dc, skip next ch-2 sp and next sc, dc2tog, ch 4, sc in next ch-2 sp, ch 4, dc2tog, ★ sc in next ch-3 sp, skip next sc, dc2tog, ch 4, sc in next ch-2 sp, ch 4, dc2tog; repeat from ★ across to last ch-2 sp, skip last ch-2 sp, sc in last dc: 33 sts and 16 ch-4 sps.

Row 4: Ch 4 (**counts as first dc plus ch 1, now and throughout**), turn; 2 dc in same st, sc in next ch-4 sp, ch 3, sc in next ch-4 sp, ★ skip next dc2tog, (2 dc, ch 2, 2 dc) in next sc, sc in next ch-4 sp, ch 3, sc in next ch-4 sp; repeat from ★ across to last 2 sts, skip next dc2tog, (2 dc, ch 1, dc) in last sc: 50 sts and 17 sps.

Row 5: Ch 1, turn; sc in first dc, ch 4, dc2tog, sc in next ch-3 sp, skip next sc, dc2tog, ch 4, ★ sc in next ch-2 sp, ch 4, dc2tog, sc in next ch-3 sp, skip next sc, dc2tog, ch 4; repeat from ★ across to last dc, sc in last dc: 33 sts and 16 ch-4 sps.

Row 6: Ch 5, turn; sc in next ch-4 sp, skip next dc2tog, (2 dc, ch 2, 2 dc) in next sc, sc in next ch-4 sp, ★ ch 3, sc in next ch-4 sp, skip next dc2tog, (2 dc, ch 2, 2 dc) in next sc, sc in next ch-4 sp; repeat from ★ across to last sc, ch 2, dc in last sc: 50 sts and 17 sps.

Rows 7-10: Repeat Rows 3-6.

Row 11: Ch 1, turn; sc in first dc, skip next ch-2 sp and next sc, dc2tog, ch 2, sc in next ch-2 sp, ch 2, dc2tog, ★ sc in next ch-3 sp, skip next sc, dc2tog, ch 2, sc in next ch-2 sp, ch 2, dc2tog; repeat from ★ across to last ch-2 sp, skip last ch-2 sp, sc in last dc: 33 sts and 16 ch-2 sps.

Row 12: Ch 1, turn; sc in first 2 sts, 2 sc in next ch-2 sp, sc in next sc, 2 sc in next ch-2 sp, sc in next dc2tog, ★ skip next sc, sc in next dc2tog, 2 sc in next ch-2 sp, sc in next sc, 2 sc in next ch-2 sp, sc in next dc2tog; repeat from ★ across to last sc, sc in last sc; do **not** finish off: 58 sc.

EDGING

Rnd 1: Ch 1, turn; 2 sc in same st, sc in each sc across to last sc, 3 sc in last sc; working in end of rows on Crown and in ▥◀ free loops of beginning ch on Back *(Fig. 3b, page 31)*, sc in next row, 2 sc in next row, (sc in next 3 rows, 2 sc in next row) twice, sc in next row and in next ch, sc2tog, (sc in next 2 chs, sc2tog) twice, sc in next ch and in next row, 2 sc in next row, (sc in next 3 rows, 2 sc in next row) twice, sc in next row and in same st as first sc; join with slip st to first sc: 99 sc.

Begin working in rows.

Row 1 (Eyelet row)**:** Ch 4, turn; skip next sc, dc in next sc, ★ ch 1, skip next sc, dc in next sc; repeat from ★ 18 times **more**, leave remaining sts unworked: 21 dc and 20 ch-1 sps.

Row 2: Ch 1, turn; sc in first dc, (4 dc in next dc, sc in next dc) across; finish off.

Weave ribbon through eyelet row.

BOOTIES
SOLE
Ch 10.

Rnd 1: 3 Sc in second ch from hook, sc in next 7 chs, 5 sc in last ch; working in ▥◀ free loops of beginning ch *(Fig. 3b, page 31)*, sc in next 7 chs, 2 sc in same ch as first sc; join with slip st to first sc: 24 sc.

Rnd 2: Ch 1, 2 sc in same st, sc in next sc, 2 sc in next sc, sc in next 7 sc, 2 sc in next sc, (sc in next sc, 2 sc in next sc) twice, sc in next 7 sc, 2 sc in next sc, sc in last sc; join with slip st to first sc: 30 sc.

Rnd 3: Ch 1, sc in same st and in next sc, † 2 sc in next sc, sc in next sc, 2 sc in next sc, sc in next 7 sc, 2 sc in next sc, sc in next sc, 2 sc in next sc †, sc in next 2 sc, repeat from † to † once; join with slip st to first sc: 38 sc.

Rnd 4: Ch 1, sc in same st and in each sc around; join with slip st to ▥◀ Back Loop Only of first sc *(Fig. 1, page 30)*, do **not** finish off.

SIDES AND INSTEP
Rnd 1: Ch 1, sc in Back Loop Only of same st and each sc around; join with slip st to **both** loops of first sc.

Rnds 2-4: Ch 1, sc in both loops of same st and each sc around; join with slip st to first sc.

Rnd 5: Ch 1, sc in same st and in next 14 sc, sc2tog 6 times, sc in last 11 sc; join with slip st to first sc: 32 sc.

Rnd 6: Ch 1, sc in same st and in next 13 sc, sc2tog, (sc in next sc, sc2tog) twice, sc in last 10 sc; join with slip st to first sc: 29 sc.

Rnd 7: Ch 1, sc in same st and in next 12 sc, sc2tog, sc in next 3 sc, sc2tog, sc in last 9 sc; join with slip st to first sc: 27 sc.

Rnd 8: Ch 1, sc in same st and in next 13 sc, pull up a loop in each of next 3 sc, YO and draw through all 4 loops on hook, sc in last 10 sc; join with slip st to first sc: 25 sts.

Rnd 9: Ch 1, sc in same st and in next 14 sts, sc2tog, sc in last 8 sc; join with slip st to first sc, do **not** finish off: 24 sc.

CUFF

Rnd 1 (Eyelet rnd)**:** Slip st in next sc, ch 4, skip next sc, ★ dc in next sc, ch 1, skip next sc; repeat from ★ around; join with slip st to third ch of beginning ch-4: 12 sts and 12 ch-1 sps.

Rnd 2: Ch 1, sc in same st and in each ch-1 sp and each dc around; join with slip st to first sc: 24 sc.

Rnd 3: Slip st in next sc, ch 1, sc in same st, ch 3, skip next sc, sc in next sc, skip next 2 sc, (2 dc, ch 2, 2 dc) in next sc, skip next 2 sc, ★ sc in next sc, ch 3, skip next sc, sc in next sc, skip next 2 sc, (2 dc, ch 2, 2 dc) in next sc, skip next 2 sc; repeat from ★ once **more**; join with slip st to first sc: 18 sts and 6 sps.

Rnd 4: Slip st in next ch-3 sp, ch 1, sc in same sp, skip next sc, dc2tog, ch 4, sc in next ch-2 sp, ch 4, dc2tog, ★ sc in next ch-3 sp, skip next sc, dc2tog, ch 4, sc in next ch-2 sp, ch 4, dc2tog; repeat from ★ once **more**; join with slip st to first sc: 12 sts and 6 ch-4 sps.

Rnd 5: Ch 3, (dc, ch 2, 2 dc) in same st, sc in next ch-4 sp, ch 3, sc in next ch-4 sp, skip next dc2tog, ★ (2 dc, ch 2, 2 dc) in next sc, sc in next ch-4 sp, ch 3, sc in next ch-4 sp, skip next dc2tog; repeat from ★ once **more**; join with slip st to top of beginning ch-3, finish off.

Weave an 18" (45.5 cm) length of ribbon through eyelet round on each Bootie.

AFGHAN
Finished Size: 38½" x 51"
  (98 cm x 129.5 cm)

AFGHAN BODY
Ch 185; place marker in fifth ch from hook for st placement.

Row 1: Sc in eighth ch from hook, skip next 2 chs, (2 dc, ch 2, 2 dc) in next ch, skip next 2 chs, sc in next ch, ★ ch 3, skip next ch, sc in next ch, skip next 2 chs, (2 dc, ch 2, 2 dc) in next ch, skip next 2 chs, sc in next ch; repeat from ★ across to last 3 chs, ch 2, skip next 2 chs, dc in last ch: 133 sts and 45 sps.

Row 2 (Right side)**:** Ch 1, turn; sc in first dc, skip next ch-2 sp and next sc, dc2tog, ch 4, sc in next ch-2 sp, ch 4, dc2tog, ★ sc in next ch-3 sp, skip next sc, dc2tog, ch 4, sc in next ch-2 sp, ch 4, dc2tog; repeat from ★ across to last sc, skip last sc and next 2 chs, sc in next ch: 89 sts and 44 sps.

Note: Loop a short piece of yarn around any stitch to mark Row 2 as **right** side.

Row 3: Ch 4 (**counts as first dc plus ch 1, now and throughout**), turn; 2 dc in same st, sc in next ch-4 sp, ch 3, sc in next ch-4 sp, skip next dc2tog, ★ (2 dc, ch 2, 2 dc) in next sc, sc in next ch-4 sp, ch 3, sc in next ch-4 sp, skip next dc2tog; repeat from ★ across to last sc, (2 dc, ch 1, dc) in last sc: 134 sts and 45 sps.

Row 4: Ch 1, turn; sc in first dc, ch 4, dc2tog, sc in next ch-3 sp, skip next sc, dc2tog, ch 4, ★ sc in next ch-2 sp, ch 4, dc2tog, sc in next ch-3 sp, skip next sc, dc2tog, ch 4; repeat from ★ across to last dc, sc in last dc: 89 sts and 44 ch-4 sps.

Row 5: Ch 5 (**counts as first dc plus ch 2**), turn; sc in next ch-4 sp, skip next dc2tog, (2 dc, ch 2, 2 dc) in next sc, sc in next ch-4 sp, ★ ch 3, sc in next ch-4 sp, skip next dc2tog, (2 dc, ch 2, 2 dc) in next sc, sc in next ch-4 sp; repeat from ★ across to last sc, ch 2, dc in last sc: 134 sts and 45 sps.

Row 6: Ch 1, turn; sc in first dc, skip next ch-2 sp and next sc, dc2tog, ch 4, sc in next ch-2 sp, ch 4, dc2tog, ★ sc in next ch-3 sp, skip next sc, dc2tog, ch 4, sc in next ch-2 sp, ch 4, dc2tog; repeat from ★ across to last ch-2 sp, skip last ch-2 sp, sc in last dc: 89 sts and 44 ch-4 sps.

Repeat Rows 3-6 until Afghan Body measures approximately 48" (122 cm) from beginning ch, ending by working Row 3.

Last Row: Ch 1, turn; sc in first dc, ch 3, dc2tog, sc in next ch-3 sp, skip next sc, dc2tog, ch 3, ★ sc in next ch-2 sp, ch 3, dc2tog, sc in next ch-3 sp, skip next sc, dc2tog, ch 3; repeat from ★ across to last dc, sc in last dc; do **not** finish off: 89 sts and 44 ch-3 sps.

EDGING

Rnd 1: Ch 1, do **not** turn; 2 sc in same st; work 207 sc  evenly spaced across end of rows to marked ch, 3 sc in marked ch; working in  free loops *(Fig. 3b, page 31)* and in sps across beginning ch, work 155 sc evenly spaced across to last ch, 3 sc in last ch; work 207 sc evenly spaced across end of rows; working across last row, 3 sc in first sc, work 155 sc evenly spaced across, sc in same st as first sc; join with slip st to first sc: 736 sc.

Rnd 2: Ch 1, 2 sc in same st, sc in each sc around working 3 sc in center sc of each corner 3-sc group, sc in same st as first sc; join with slip st to first sc: 744 sc.

Rnd 3 (Eyelet rnd)**:** Ch 4, (dc, ch 1) twice in same st, skip next sc, (dc in next sc, ch 1, skip next sc) across to center sc of next corner 3-sc group, ★ (dc, ch 1) 3 times in center sc, skip next sc, (dc in next sc, ch 1, skip next sc) across to center sc of next corner 3-sc group; repeat from ★ 2 times **more**; join with slip st to first dc: 380 dc and 380 ch-1 sps.

Rnd 4: Ch 1, sc in same st and in each ch-1 sp and each dc around working 3 sc in center dc of each corner 3-dc group; join with slip st to first sc: 768 sc.

Rnd 5: Ch 1, sc in same st, skip next 2 sc, 8 dc in center sc, skip next 2 sc, ★ sc in next sc, (skip next sc, 4 dc in next sc, skip next sc, sc in next sc) across to within 2 sc of center sc of next corner 3-sc group, skip next 2 sc, 8 dc in center sc, skip next 2 sc; repeat from ★ 2 times **more**, (sc in next sc, skip next sc, 4 dc in next sc, skip next sc) across; join with slip st to first sc, finish off.

Beginning at any corner, weave ribbon through eyelet round of Edging and tie ends into a bow.

ABBREVIATIONS

BPdc	Back Post double crochet(s)
ch(s)	chain(s)
dc	double crochet(s)
dc2tog	double crochet 2 together
FPdc	Front Post double crochet(s)
hdc	half double crochet(s)
mm	millimeters
Rnd(s)	Round(s)
sc	single crochet(s)
sc2tog	single crochet 2 together
sp(s)	space(s)
st(s)	stitch(es)
YO	yarn over

SYMBOLS & TERMS

★ — work instructions following ★ as many **more** times as indicated in addition to the first time.

† to † — work all instructions from first † to second † **as many** times as specified.

( ) or [ ] — work enclosed instructions **as many** times as specified by the number immediately following **or** work all enclosed instructions in the stitch or space indicated **or** contains explanatory remarks.

colon (:) — the number(s) given after a colon at the end of a row or round denote(s) the number of stitches or spaces you should have on that row or round.

CROCHET TERMINOLOGY

UNITED STATES		INTERNATIONAL
slip stitch (slip st)	=	single crochet (sc)
single crochet (sc)	=	double crochet (dc)
half double crochet (hdc)	=	half treble crochet (htr)
double crochet (dc)	=	treble crochet(tr)
treble crochet (tr)	=	double treble crochet (dtr)
double treble crochet (dtr)	=	triple treble crochet (ttr)
triple treble crochet (tr tr)	=	quadruple treble crochet (qtr)
skip	=	miss

Yarn Weight Symbol & Names	LACE 0	SUPER FINE 1	FINE 2	LIGHT 3	MEDIUM 4	BULKY 5	SUPER BULKY 6
Type of Yarns in Category	Fingering, 10-count crochet thread	Sock, Fingering Baby	Sport, Baby	DK, Light Worsted	Worsted, Afghan, Aran	Chunky, Craft, Rug	Bulky, Roving
Crochet Gauge* Ranges in Single Crochet to 4" (10 cm)	32-42 double crochets**	21-32 sts	16-20 sts	12-17 sts	11-14 sts	8-11 sts	5-9 sts
Advised Hook Size Range	Steel*** 6,7,8 Regular hook B-1	B-1 to E-4	E-4 to 7	7 to I-9	I-9 to K-10.5	K-10.5 to M-13	M-13 and larger

*GUIDELINES ONLY: The chart above reflects the most commonly used gauges and hook sizes for specific yarn categories.

** Lace weight yarns are usually crocheted on larger-size hooks to create lacy openwork patterns. Accordingly, a gauge range is difficult to determine. Always follow the gauge stated in your pattern.

*** Steel crochet hooks are sized differently from regular hooks–the higher the number the smaller the hook, which is the reverse of regular hook sizing.

GAUGE

Exact gauge is **essential** for proper size. Before beginning your project, make the sample swatch given in the individual instructions in the yarn and hook specified. After completing the swatch, measure it, counting your stitches and rows or rounds carefully. If your swatch is larger or smaller than specified, **make another, changing hook size to get the correct gauge.** Keep trying until you find the size hook that will give you the specified gauge.

JOINING WITH SC

When instructed to join with sc, begin with a slip knot on hook. Insert hook in stitch or space indicated, YO and pull up a loop, YO and draw through both loops on hook.

BACK OR FRONT LOOP ONLY

Work only in loop(s) indicated by arrow *(Fig. 1)*.

Fig. 1

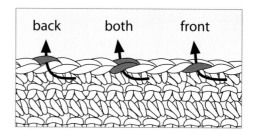

BACK RIDGE

Work only in loops indicated by arrows *(Fig. 2)*.

Fig. 2

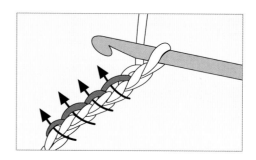

CROCHET HOOKS																
U.S.	B-1	C-2	D-3	E-4	F-5	G-6	7	H-8	I-9	J-10	K-10½	L-11	M/N-13	N/P-15	P/Q	Q	S
Metric - mm	2.25	2.75	3.25	3.5	3.75	4	4.5	5	5.5	6	6.5	8	9	10	15	16	19

◼◻◻◻ **BEGINNER**	Projects for first-time crocheters using basic stitches. Minimal shaping.
◼◼◻◻ **EASY**	Projects using yarn with basic stitches, repetitive stitch patterns, simple color changes, and simple shaping and finishing.
◼◼◼◻ **INTERMEDIATE**	Projects using a variety of techniques, such as basic lace patterns or color patterns, mid-level shaping and finishing.
◼◼◼◼ **EXPERIENCED**	Projects with intricate stitch patterns, techniques and dimension, such as non-repeating patterns, multi-color techniques, fine threads, small hooks, detailed shaping and refined finishing.

FREE LOOPS

After working in Back or Front Loops Only on a row or round, there will be a ridge of unused loops. These are called the free loops. Later, when instructed to work in the free loops of the same row or round, work in these loops (Fig. 3a).

When instructed to work in free loops of a chain, work in loop(s) indicated by arrow (Fig. 3b or 3c).

Fig. 3a

Fig. 3b

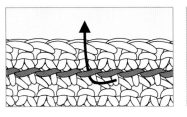

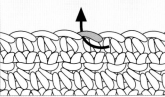

Fig. 3c

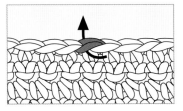

POST STITCH

Work around post of stitch indicated, inserting hook in direction of arrow (Fig. 4).

Fig. 4

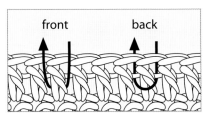

POM-POM

Cut a piece of cardboard 3" (7.5 cm) wide and as long as you want the diameter of your finished pom-pom to be. Wind the yarn around the cardboard until it is approximately ½" (12 mm) thick in the middle (Fig. 5a). Carefully slip the yarn off the cardboard and firmly tie an 18" (45.5 cm) length of yarn around the middle (Fig. 5b). Leave yarn ends long enough to attach the pom-pom. Cut the loops on both ends and trim the pom-pom into a smooth ball (Fig. 5c).

Fig. 5a

Fig. 5b

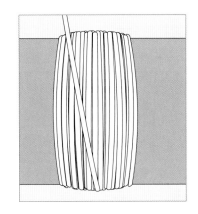

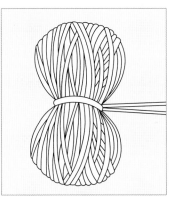

Fig. 5c

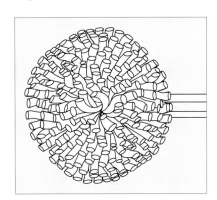

Yarn Infomation

The items in this book were made using Light Weight Yarn. Any LIght Weight Yarn may be used. It is best to refer to the yardage/meters when determining how many balls or skeins to purchase. Remember, to arrive at the finished size, it is the GAUGE/TENSION that is important, not the brand of yarn.

For your convenience, listed below are the specific yarns used to create our photography models.

PINK SET

Lion Brand® Babysoft®

Pink - #101 Pastel Pink

White - #100 White

GREEN SET

Lion Brand® Babysoft®

Green - # 156 Pastel Green

White - #100 White

WHITE SET

Lion Brand® Babysoft®

#100 White

BLUE SET

Patons® Astra

#08737 Ocean Mist

We have made every effort to ensure that these instructions are accurate and complete. We cannot, however, be responsible for human error, typographical mistakes, or variations in individual work.

Production Team: Technical Writer/ Editor - Lois J. Long; Senior Graphic Artist - Lora Puls; Graphic Artist - Jessica Bramlett; Photo Stylist - Sondra Daniel; and Photographer - Ken West.